CONTE

INTRODUCTION

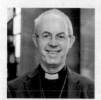 

In times of storm, when there is chaos and danger all around us, it is good to set our feet on rock. For all Christians, the creed is that solid ground. Whenever we say "I believe in God" in public or in private we are placing trust once more in God's grace and goodness revealed in Christ, whatever might be happening in the world around us.

From earliest times, Christians have summarized and recited what we believe in short forms, often learned by heart. The Apostles' Creed is the best known of these summaries.

Pilgrim Journeys invites you to spend 40 days reflecting on more of what these words mean.

Our hope and prayer is that these reflections will be helpful to many people as they make the journey to baptism and confirmation, providing a strong and deep foundation for faith and discipleship.

But any Christian will be blessed by revisiting the core and centre of the faith again and seeing these ancient truths in fresh ways. You may want to use these reflections in Lent – the traditional time when Christians prepare for and reflect on baptism – but they can be read with profit at any time of the year.

However you read this *Pilgrim Journey*, welcome. May Christ give you strength as you follow with us the Way of Jesus.

Archbishops Justin Welby and Stephen Cottrell

HOW TO USE THIS BOOK

Pilgrim Journeys: The Creeds can be used at any time of year but is ideal for anyone to use daily during Lent – starting from Ash Wednesday* and either finishing 40 days later on Palm Sunday (if you use it every day) or on Easter Eve (if you use it every day except Sunday).

Those preparing for baptism, confirmation or the renewal of baptism promises may find it helpful as part of their preparation for that commitment. Members of *Pilgrim* groups who are spending six weeks exploring *The Creeds* (Book 5) together may find it helpful to use this daily material in between sessions.

The 40 daily reflections on The Apostles' Creed are grouped in eight chapters of five days. Each day offers:

- A **theme** linked to a section of The Apostles' Creed
- A short Bible **reading** that explores that theme
- An invitation to **reflect** on the reading
- A prompt to **pause** and consider what this might mean for you
- A suggestion of how to **pray**.

Across each group of five days we will explore what each section of The Apostles' Creed means for us, for our faith and for how we live it out in everyday life.

At the end, you will find some possible next steps for you on your discipleship journey, as well as some further resources including other *Pilgrim* materials for you to explore.

* Ash Wednesday falls on the following dates over the coming years:
17 February in 2021; 2 March in 2022; 22 February in 2023;
14 February in 2024; 5 March in 2025; 18 February in 2026.

A SHORT GUIDE TO THE APOSTLES' CREED

The Pilgrim Way: A short guide to the Christian Faith explores what it means to share and live out our faith and identity as followers of Jesus Christ. It is shaped around four core Christian texts, including The Apostles' Creed.

This extract from *The Pilgrim Way* summarizes what this ancient statement of Christian belief – handed down through the ages – means for the Church of today.

You might like to read this before you embark on the daily reflections, and perhaps re-visit it each week, or even try learning it by heart.

. . . .

Pilgrim, what is the faith of the Church?

The faith of the Church is revealed in the Holy Scriptures and set forth in the words of the Apostles' Creed.

. . . .

THE APOSTLES' CREED

I believe in God, the Father almighty,
creator of heaven and earth.

I believe in Jesus Christ,
his only Son, our Lord,
who was conceived by the Holy Spirit,
born of the Virgin Mary,
suffered under Pontius Pilate,
was crucified, died, and was buried;
he descended to the dead.
On the third day he rose again;
he ascended into heaven,
he is seated at the right hand
of the Father,
and he will come to judge
the living and the dead.

I believe in the Holy Spirit,
the holy catholic Church,
the communion of saints,
the forgiveness of sins,
the resurrection of the body,
and the life everlasting.
Amen.

What does it mean to believe in one God: Father, Son and Holy Spirit? To believe is to trust in the Father's love for the world, in the saving work of Jesus Christ on the cross, and in the transforming power of the Holy Spirit.

. . . .

How do you become a Christian? By turning to Jesus Christ in faith, by repenting of your sin, and being baptized in the name of the Father and of the Son and of the Holy Spirit.

. . . .

What is sin? Sin means not living according to the will of God. To sin is to fall short in our thoughts, words and deeds, through what we do and through what we fail to do. Sin separates us from God and neighbour.

. . . .

What is baptism? Baptism in water is the sacrament of new birth in Christ. We die to sin that we may live his risen life. We are washed by the Holy Spirit and become members of the Church.

. . . .

What is the Church? The Church is the pilgrim people of God, the body of Christ, and the community of disciples in every age in earth and heaven.

DAYS 1 TO 5

**'I BELIEVE
IN GOD'**

DAY 1
ON GOD ALONE

READ Psalm 62.1–7

'On God alone my soul in stillness waits; from him comes my salvation.'

. . . .

REFLECT

Christians believe amazing things. These wonderful truths have been distilled into the Apostles' Creed. Every act in the drama of salvation is here forged into a strong, life-saving and life-giving chain.

Over the next 40 days we will relive this great drama. If you are new to the faith, open your eyes to the wonder of what Christians believe.

If you have been a Christian for many years, come back to the very centre. Take these mighty truths and place them at the very core of your heart and life: a resounding echo of the living Word of God: Jesus Christ.

The opening words of the creed are words of power: I believe in God.

Whenever we say those words we are standing again in the place of our baptism: we put our trust in God alone for our life and our eternal life. We place ourselves within God's story. We return to the very centre of our lives.

. . . .

PAUSE

How will you set aside time and space for reflection and listening through these 40 days?

. . . .

PRAY

In God is my strength and my glory;
God is my strong rock; in him is my refuge.
Psalm 62

DAY 2
GOD'S CALL

READ Genesis 15.1–6

*'And Abraham believed the Lord;
and the Lord reckoned it to him
as righteousness.'*

. . . .

REFLECT

The Book of Genesis unfolds a life-changing
mystery: Almighty God, maker of the universe, calls
men and women to know him. God reveals himself
in many different ways first through calling a single
family, the family of Abraham, who become in time
a single nation, Israel. From that nation God will
bring blessing to the whole world.

God does not choose Abraham or Sarah because of their special goodness. No one in all of this imperfect creation is good enough to be able to know God. God calls Abraham because of his faith: because Abraham and Sarah are able to say, in time, 'I believe' and to follow where God leads.

We can know God only by trusting God. To say, 'I believe' in the great trials and difficulties of our lives is to place our trust again in God's existence and God's goodness and God's call: to choose to see the world as ultimately good and purposeful. Faith is still reckoned to us as righteousness.

. . . .

PAUSE

What are the times in your life when your faith has been most confident?

. . . .

PRAY

Make these words – first spoken by the father who had begged Jesus to heal his son – your prayer today:

'I believe. Help my unbelief.'
Mark 9.24

DAY 3
STEPPING INTO GOD'S STORY

READ Deuteronomy 26.1–11

' … so now I bring the first fruits of the ground that you, O Lord, have given me.'

. . . .

REFLECT

God calls Abraham, a wandering Aramean. Abraham went down to Egypt and became father to a great nation. God delivered the nation from slavery and brought them to freedom in the promised land.

Every generation of God's people needs to remember this long story (and there are other chapters still to come). But every generation needs also to make this story their own story: to stand within the long history of the people of God.

This is what is happening here in this simple ritual. Every person, in every generation, takes some of the first fruits of the harvest and brings it before God as an offering and makes a confession of faith before God and before the people.

This is what is happening when Christians declare our faith in the words of the Apostles' Creed. We too are stepping into God's story and making that story our own. We are remaking and re-membering the people of God in our own generation and becoming part of the chain of faith ourselves.

· ·

PAUSE

In your own life, who are your ancestors in faith and heroes and heroines in the faith?

· ·

PRAY

Give thanks for all those who have helped to pass on the Christian faith to you and helped you to make it your own.

DAY 4
GOOD NEWS

READ 1 Corinthians 15.1–11

'Last of all, as to someone untimely born, he appeared also to me.'

. . . .

REFLECT

Paul offers one of the very earliest summaries of the good news: an early creed. Christ died for our sins, was buried and was raised on the third day in accordance with the Scriptures.

Through Christ, God's call now comes to everyone in every nation. The power of declaring our faith in God through Christ is immense.

Abraham is justified with God through faith: when he says 'I believe.' Paul is justified with God through faith when he says: 'I believe' on the Damascus road. You and I are made right with God not because of our inherent goodness or because of the good deeds we do but when we say and mean these great words of power: 'I believe and trust in him.'

Every time we say the first line of the Apostles' Creed we echo the declaration of faith made at our baptism. These are words of great life and power.

. . . .

PAUSE

Are you able to tell – or show – someone today that you believe and trust in God?

. . . .

PRAY

Make these words – spoken by new Christians at the service of Baptism – your prayer today:

I believe and trust in him.
Common Worship Baptism Service

MY LORD AND MY GOD

READ John 20.24–31

'Blessed are those who have not seen and yet have come to believe.'

. . . .

REFLECT

The journey of faith is not always easy. Thomas initially refuses to believe the news of Jesus' resurrection. Jesus deals patiently with him and calls Thomas to a still deeper encounter. This deeper encounter draws an even deeper response: my Lord and my God. It is Thomas who comes to faith more slowly who sees more clearly who Jesus really is.

Jesus deals gently with his disciple but saves a blessing for us: those who have not seen and yet have come to believe. The chain of believing begins with Abraham and continues through the people of Israel, to the first disciples, to the early church and down the generations to you and me today. God still calls and saves and shapes and remakes us.

The Apostles' Creed we are exploring together summarizes and unfolds these wonderful truths at the heart of God's call and God's salvation. As we respond to God in the creed's opening words, we stand in this long, deep, worldwide tradition of believing.

. . . .

PAUSE

Who are your great heroines and heroes of faith in the Scriptures and Church history?

. . . .

PRAY

Pray today using Thomas's words, repeating them slowly:

'My Lord and my God.'
John 20.28

DAYS 6 TO 10
'THE FATHER
ALMIGHTY,
CREATOR OF
HEAVEN AND
EARTH'

WHEN I CONSIDER YOUR HEAVENS ...

READ Psalm 8

'What are mortals that you should be mindful of them? Mere human beings that you should seek them out?'

. . . .

REFLECT

The universe is immense and beautiful and ordered and ancient. Our eyes might be caught by the swirling patterns of a galaxy or the hidden language of trees. We might explore the wonder of microbes or the joy of observing a hippo bathing or a red kite hovering over the fields.

Sooner or later, everyone who explores the universe will return to the question: why are we here? Who generated this order and beauty and life? What is my place as a person within this vast creation? What is the place of humankind?

The Apostles' Creed unfolds and structures our faith and understanding. The first line is simple and bold:

I believe in God. This faith in God is then explored in three strands as faith in Father, Son and Holy Spirit: Almighty God in an everlasting Trinity of love – love which overflows in creation, salvation and in making all things new.

Who are we? Our answer to the question flows from our faith.

. . . .

PAUSE

Notice the wonder of creation today in the daylight and in the evening.

. . . .

PRAY

Pray today using the words of praise with which Psalm 8 begin and ends:

O Lord, our governor, how glorious is your name in all the world.
Psalm 8.1

FATHER, SON AND HOLY SPIRIT

READ Ephesians 1.3-14

'Blessed be the God and Father of our Lord Jesus Christ, who has blessed us in Christ with every spiritual blessing in the heavenly places ... '

. . . .

REFLECT

The Apostles' Creed tells us just two things about the first person of the Trinity. First, God is the Father almighty. Second, God is creator of heaven and earth. It's important to get these two truths in the right order.

The creation is the overflow of God's love. God's love is shown first in the love of the Father for the Son and the Spirit. In love, in generosity, God makes the heavens and the earth and all that is from nothing. In the same love and generosity, God sustains the universe and all that is in the universe moment by moment.

The great blessing in Ephesians 1 draws back the curtain on God's purposes of love: God the Father has blessed us in Christ with every spiritual blessing in the heavenly places: in our creation, preservation and all the blessings of this life. The Father and the Son have given us the Holy Spirit to dwell within us. The centre of our lives and calling is to join this eternal circle of love to the praise of God's glory.

PAUSE

Practise thanksgiving today as your response to God's love as Father and Creator.

PRAY

Offer your thanksgiving for God's love today in the opening words of today's reading:

Blessed be the God and Father of our Lord Jesus Christ ...
Ephesians 1.3

DAY 8
IN THE BEGINNING ...

READ Genesis 1.1-9, 12-19

'In the beginning when God created the heavens and the earth, the earth was a formless void ... '

. . . .

REFLECT

Christians see God the Trinity active in creation. God creates by his Word, the Son. God's Spirit, or wind, broods over the face of the waters to bring life. God orders the entire universe and God's creation is good and very good.

The great advances of science mean we see the universe differently now with greater humility. Our fragile planet Earth is not the centre of everything. If the life of our planet is a single day, what we know as human history is four seconds before midnight.

But we also know that life is at the very least rare in the universe. It is possible that life on earth is unique. We are the only part of creation able to see creation and understand it and give thanks to the creator. We place our trust in God, Father Almighty, creator of heaven and earth, the origin of life and power and goodness and order.

. . . .

PAUSE

List before God today the parts of creation you find most beautiful and full of wonder.

. . . .

PRAY

Not to us, Lord, not to us,
but to your name give the glory,
for the sake of your loving mercy and truth.
Psalm 115.1

THE IMAGE OF GOD

READ Genesis 1.26—2.3

'So God created humankind in his image; in the image of God he created them; male and female he created them.'

. . . .

REFLECT

Psalm 8 (which we read on Day 6) looks at the universe and asks the profound question: what does it mean to be human? Genesis 1 offers an answer. The words are to be read as full of wonder.

First, there is the order of creation from abstract concepts to inanimate matter: to plants, to fish, to the birds of the air and creeping things. And there is humankind: the pinnacle of all creation, made on the sixth day.

Second, out of all creation only humankind is made in the image and likeness of God: there is a spark of the divine in men and women seen most powerfully in our ability to love and to be loved, to wonder, to reason and to return thanks to our creator.

Third, there is the blessing and command to be fruitful, to multiply, to fill the earth and be good stewards (a better translation than 'subdue'). God looks at all that God has made and behold it is indeed very good.

. . . .

PAUSE

Review the actions you need to take as a steward of creation to help care for creation in this critical generation.

. . . .

PRAY

We bless you, master of the heavens, for the wonderful order which enfolds this world …
Common Worship Psalm Prayer for Psalm 8

THE WORD MADE FLESH

READ John 1.1-14

'And the Word became flesh and lived among us, and we have seen his glory, the glory as of a father's only son, full of grace and truth.'

. . . .

REFLECT

John's gospel is written to open our eyes to the truth about Jesus. The Word of God simply was in the beginning with God, before time, before creation, before there was a before. The Son is not part of the creation but the agent of creation with the Father and the Holy Spirit.

The Word of God, this agent of creation, was always in the world, God's reason permeating every rock and flower, every grain of sand, sustaining every part of the universe. But the world did not recognise him. Human beings could see only glimpses of God's eternal wonder. The Son did not enter the creation when Jesus was born: the Son was always in the world and always weaving patterns of love.

God's living Word takes human form, creator in creation in a new and focused way in Jesus. Only in this way are we able to see and know the Father, creator of heaven and earth.

. . . .

PAUSE

Open your eyes today to the presence of God's reason and presence in creation.

. . . .

PRAY

Almighty God, who wonderfully created us in your own image and yet more wonderfully restored us through your Son Jesus Christ: grant that, as he came to share in our humanity, so may we share the life of his divinity ...
Collect for the First Sunday of Christmas

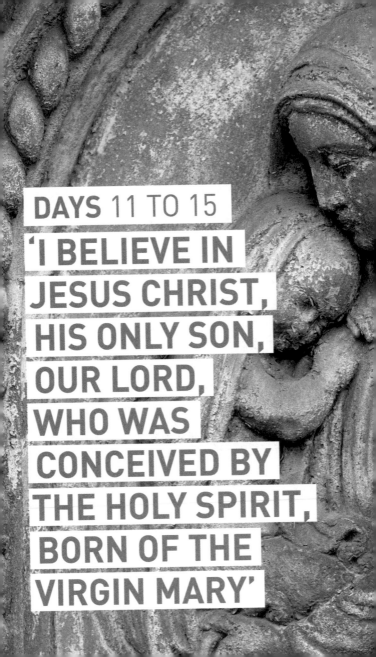

DAYS 11 TO 15

'I BELIEVE IN JESUS CHRIST, HIS ONLY SON, OUR LORD, WHO WAS CONCEIVED BY THE HOLY SPIRIT, BORN OF THE VIRGIN MARY'

DAY 11
YOU ARE MY SON
READ Psalm 2

'I will proclaim the decree of the Lord;
he said to me: "You are my Son; this
day have I begotten you." '

. . . .

REFLECT

The central question of our age is what does it
mean to be human? The question is asked by the
climate emergency: the story of Planet Earth and of
our species has reached a crossroads in our own
lifetime. The question is asked by the extraordinary
technology available to us – and its future trajectory.

Christians believe amazing things and at the very
centre of our faith is this extraordinary and world
defining truth. We believe that Almighty God, creator
of heaven and earth, became a single human person
in one time and place. We believe that Jesus Christ,
the child born in Bethlehem, is the eternal Son of
God, the divine Word.

The incarnation of the Son of God grows out of the deep longing in the Old Testament for God's new anointed king, or Christ, who will bring about a kingdom of justice and peace. For 42 generations, God prepared the way for the coming of his Son through prophets, kings and psalmists. What does this mean for all of humankind?

. . . .

PAUSE

Research and make a note of the different titles for Jesus in the Old Testament and the New.

. . . .

PRAY

Lord Jesus Christ, your birth at Bethlehem draws us to kneel in wonder at heaven touching earth: accept our heartfelt praise as we worship you, our Saviour and our eternal God.

Additional Collect for Christmas Day

DAY 12
THE BIRTH OF JESUS CHRIST

READ Matthew 1.18-25

'She will bear a son, and you are to name him Jesus, for he will save his people from their sins.'

. . . .

REFLECT

The Christmas story is so familiar that we miss the deep mysteries it holds. God's own Son takes flesh in the body of a young woman. Mary's role in the story of salvation is so significant that she is one of only two people named in the Apostles' Creed.

Both the creed and the gospel story bear witness to Christ's humanity and Christ's divinity. Jesus' very conception is from the Holy Spirit yet the Son of God arrives as a vulnerable child born in a normal way. Mary is a virgin when the child is conceived, fulfilling the ancient prophecy from Isaiah (Chapters 7 and 9). But her Son is born into a very human family.

From before his birth, the child is named as 'Jesus', in Hebrew the new Joshua, because he will save his people from their sins. The child fulfils the prophecies of Scripture – here that he will be called Emmanuel, God with us. At the very beginning of his story, we ask over and over again, Who is this Jesus?

. . . .

PAUSE

Mary's vocation is to say yes to God's call. What do you understand God's call to be on your own life?

. . . .

PRAY

Pray today using Mary's words in response to God's call: 'Here am I, the servant of the Lord; let it be with me according to your word.' **Luke 1.38**

SON OF DAVID, SON OF GOD

READ Romans 1.1-7

' ... the gospel concerning his Son, who was descended from David according to the flesh and was declared to be Son of God ... '

. . . .

REFLECT

The letters in the New Testament were mainly written before the gospels. From the very earliest times, Christians see Jesus as both fully human and fully God. Paul expresses this truth in Romans 1 in a careful, balanced way. Jesus is descended from David according to the flesh. He is the fulfilment of Israel's hope for an anointed king, a Messiah or Christ.

Jesus is declared to be the unique Son of God with power, conceived by the Holy Spirit. His divine nature is revealed by his resurrection from the dead. Only this way of seeing Jesus Christ makes sense of all the evidence around his birth, his ministry, his teaching, his character, his miracles, his death, his resurrection.

The Church will debate for many centuries the best way to express these wonderful truths. The longer Nicene Creed adds more articles here (see the prayer below). All creeds preserve this central balance of the incarnation: Jesus is fully human, fully God.

. . . .

PAUSE

Reflect on what difference it makes to your relationship with Jesus Christ that he is fully human and fully God.

. . . .

PRAY

Use these articles of the Nicene Creed as a hymn of praise to Jesus:

the only Son of God,
eternally begotten of the Father,
God from God, Light from Light ...

DAY 14
WHO IS THIS?

READ Mark 4.35-41

'Who then is this that even the wind and the sea obey him?'

. . . .

REFLECT

Every page and passage in the gospels asks the question: 'Who is this?' The four gospels are written to provoke our curiosity and to unfold the evidence. We enter into the experiences of the very first disciples, see what they witness and wonder with them about the unique nature of Christ.

Some passages in the gospels reveal the humanity of Jesus: he loves and weeps and serves and is hurt.

Some passages reveal his divinity.

In this passage, Jesus is on the one hand exhausted so as to be able to sleep through a storm. On the other he is able to still that same storm by his power. In the Bible's world view, the sea represents the forces of chaos and darkness, beyond human control. The stilling is the evidence that even the forces of chaos and confusion are ordered and re-ordered by a word spoken by the Son of God. Who is this? Our friend. The maker of heaven and earth.

PAUSE

Take some time to identify the storms and forces of chaos in your own life. Invite Jesus in.

PRAY

Use these articles of the Nicene Creed as a hymn of praise to Jesus:

begotten not made,
of one being with the Father
through him all things were made

DO YOU WANT TO BE MADE WELL?

READ John 5.1-9

'At once the man was made well and he took up his mat and began to walk.'

. . . .

REFLECT

The creed unfolds the drama of salvation. The Son of God takes flesh, born for our salvation. At every line, this gospel invites a response.

We can spend the whole of our lives knowing but not understanding the truth of the gospel. It is as though we lie by the pool, blind, lame and paralysed. The human condition is that we cannot help ourselves or rescue ourselves. We have no-one to bring us to the waters when they are stirred up.

Jesus the Good Shepherd comes to seek us out among the crowd. He knows our story and our condition. He draws alongside and gently asks us: 'Do you want to be made well?'

His questions invite a response and the response is the simple trust of faith: I believe and trust in him. We are not made well because of our gifts or good deeds or anything else we bring. We are saved by grace through faith in Christ: through the power of trust. The creed is the pathway to life.

. . . .

PAUSE

Imagine yourself in the scene in the gospel story and imagine Jesus asks you the same question. How do you reply?

. . . .

PRAY

Do you believe and trust in God the Son
who took our human nature,
died for us and rose again?

I believe and trust in him.
Common Worship Affirmation of Faith

DAYS 16 TO 20

'SUFFERED UNDER PONTIUS PILATE, WAS CRUCIFIED, DIED, AND WAS BURIED; HE DESCENDED TO THE DEAD'

DAY 16
POURED OUT LIKE WATER

READ Psalm 22.1-15

'My God, my God, why have you forsaken me, and are so far from my salvation, from the words of my distress?'

. . . .

REFLECT

God the maker and creator becomes a person to show our worth and value, to model what it is to be human, to show us how to live our lives in love and service and to lead us back to love of God and love of neighbour. So far this is a wonderful and comfortable creed.

But now there is a more difficult turn. God's own Son did not only live. God's Son came to die. Jesus experienced the whole of what it means to be human, not just the 'nice' parts. Jesus experienced suffering, injustice, rejection and death.

Understanding this part of the mystery takes us first to its roots in the Psalms. The anointed king in the Psalms experiences deep suffering, sometimes, as here, taking into himself the profound suffering of the nation in times of siege, starvation and destruction.

Jesus quotes Psalm 22 from the cross, identifying with this deep tradition of the leader who suffers with and for his people. God is with us in the darkness. No pain or sorrow is beyond his love.

PAUSE

Look back over your life. When has the death of Jesus seemed most real and most important to you?

PRAY

O God, our sovereign and shepherd,
who brought again your Son Jesus Christ
from the valley of death,
comfort us with your protecting presence
this day and all days.
Common Worship Psalm Prayer for Psalm 23

DAY 17
THE PASSION OF THE LORD

READ Mark 15.1-20

'And the soldiers began saluting him, "Hail, King of the Jews!" '

. . . .

REFLECT

Christians have a special word for the suffering of Jesus and the parts of the gospel which describe his arrest, trial and death. We call his suffering his Passion and these chapters of the gospels are the passion narratives.

The word Passion has two meanings here. These are stories of great suffering (the first meaning) as power, reputation, friendship and dignity are stripped away. They are also stories of great love (the second) as each gospel makes clear that Jesus goes willingly to his death and sees in his sacrifice great blessing and meaning for all the world.

Jesus fulfils the great prophecies of the Scriptures as he comes as king, yet he comes as a king who will suffer for the sins of his people in order to heal them. The people he comes to save are not particularly good or loveable – quite the opposite. They are those who mock and crucify him. So great is his Passion.

. . . .

PAUSE

Read this part of the Passion story again slowly and carefully and notice the love and gentleness of the Son of God.

. . . .

PRAY

We adore you, O Christ, and we bless you, because by your holy cross you have redeemed the world.
Prayer During the Day for Passiontide

DAY 18
GOD'S SON

READ Mark 15.21-41

'Now when the centurion, who stood facing him, saw that in this way he breathed his last he said, "Truly this man was God's Son!" '

. . . .

REFLECT

Mark asks the question from the beginning of the gospel to the end: who is this Jesus? The clearest answer comes at the moment of Jesus' crucifixion and death from the Gentile centurion who oversees his execution. Christ's tortured body hangs naked on the cross. In that moment the centurion recognizes his divinity.

The Son of God has taken flesh, born of Mary, has lived and loved and taught and healed and has been crucified. Jesus lived in history and his death is an historical event, attested by Roman soldiers who knew their job. His body is taken from the cross by his friends, wrapped in a linen cloth and laid in a tomb hewn from the rock.

In response to his death, Christians take as our central act of worship the breaking of bread to remember his body broken here and the sharing of a cup of wine to remember his blood, his life's force, poured out for many for the forgiveness of sins.

. . . .

PAUSE

Find and read one of the prayers of thanksgiving said at Holy Communion. What do you learn here about the death of Jesus?

. . . .

PRAY

We glory in your cross, O Lord, and praise and glorify your holy resurrection: for by virtue of the cross joy has come to the whole world.
Prayer During the Day for Passiontide

HEALING AND SALVATION

READ Isaiah 53.1-9

'But he was wounded for our trans-gressions ... upon him was the punishment that made us whole, and by his bruises we are healed.'

. . . .

REFLECT

The longer Nicene Creed says this of Jesus: "For us and for our salvation he came down from heaven". Salvation is accomplished through the whole of Jesus' life and ministry but especially through his death on the cross for the sins of the whole world.

Again, the meaning of his death is foretold in the Scriptures. The prophet who speaks in the beautiful servant songs of Isaiah 40-55 dwells on the suffering servant and the meaning of that suffering: in his wounds we find our healing, the punishment that makes us whole, the propitiation for all our sins.

The creeds are careful not to describe exactly how the suffering and death of Jesus atone for our sins. Different images are helpful but each falls short. The creeds invite us, week by week, simply to place our faith and trust in the power of his death to bring forgiveness and new life. The testimony of the Church through the ages is that such faith transforms us.

. . . .

PAUSE

Take some time to bring all of your shortcomings and sins afresh to God and seek forgiveness through the death of Jesus.

. . . .

PRAY

Lord Jesus Christ,
Son of the living God,
have mercy on me, a sinner.
The Jesus Prayer

THE RIGHTEOUSNESS FROM GOD

READ Philippians 3.7-16

'I want to know Christ and the power of his resurrection and the sharing of his sufferings by becoming like him in his death ...'

. . . .

REFLECT

It is our privilege as Christians to receive the benefits of the cross in the forgiveness of our sins, in the renewal of our lives and in the resurrection from the dead. However believing in the death of Jesus on the cross is about more than accepting these blessings.

For Christ comes also to model a way of life and the cross becomes a pattern for the life of every disciple. This is so in the teachings of Jesus in the gospels and the invitation to take up our own cross. It is a strong theme in the writings of Paul whose deepest aspiration is to become like him in his death and know the fellowship of suffering.

This set of spectacles really does turn the world upside down. Ambition is subverted to service. Suffering is transfigured into discipleship. Weakness is tempered into strength sufficient to change the world. The way of death becomes the way of life.

. . . .

PAUSE

Spend a few moments reflecting on the presence of suffering in your life in this season. How can it be transfigured into the path of discipleship?

. . . .

PRAY

Almighty God,
whose most dear Son went not up to joy
but first he suffered pain,
and entered not into glory
before he was crucified:
mercifully grant that we,
walking in the way of the cross,
may find it none other
than the way of life and peace.
Collect for the Third Sunday of Lent

'ON THE THIRD DAY
HE ROSE AGAIN;
HE ASCENDED INTO
HEAVEN, HE IS
SEATED AT THE
RIGHT HAND OF
THE FATHER,
HE WILL COME TO
JUDGE THE LIVING
AND THE DEAD'

DAY 21
DELIVERED FROM DEATH

READ Psalm 116.1-9

'For you have delivered my soul from death, my eyes from tears and my feet from falling.'

· ·

REFLECT

Christians believe amazing things. As we come to the centre of the creed we arrive at the place where eternity and creation intersect: Jesus is crucified but on the third day rises from the dead. The tomb is empty. The risen Christ appears to his disciples. Death and entropy are reversed. The whole creation is caught up in almighty Alleluias.

This too is according to the Scriptures. The early Christians quoted Psalm 116 as evidence that the Son of God could not be held by death. The Psalm is the prayer of one who has faced death but has lived, a song of thanksgiving for great deliverance.

The resurrection, like the cross, is a truth for all people everywhere. It is not simply a profound truth for Jesus: this one man was raised from the dead and lives for ever. As his death holds meaning for everyone, so does this one resurrection. Because he lives, we will live.

. . . .

PAUSE

Sit quietly and reflect for some moments on the glorious hope of the resurrection of the dead. Then take this powerful hope with you into your day and notice the difference it makes.

. . . .

PRAY

As we walk through the valley of the shadow of death, may we call upon your name, raise the cup of salvation, and so proclaim your death, O Lord, until you come in glory.
Common Worship Psalm Prayer for Psalm 116

DAY 22
RESURRECTION

READ John 20.11-23

'Mary Magdalene went and announced to the disciples, "I have seen the Lord." '

. . . .

REFLECT

How do we know and understand and believe that Jesus is risen? How are we able to say these lines of the creed with confidence?

The primary reason is the testimony of witnesses in a long series beginning with Mary Magdalene, then Peter and the other apostles, then more than five hundred gathered together at one time. These eyewitness accounts are preserved in the gospels which together make the astonishing claim that Jesus of Nazareth rose from the dead.

The testimony of the eyewitnesses is supplemented by the historical evidence of the empty tomb. The first disciples were transformed by their encounters from deserters to those who gave their lives for their faith. Most powerfully, we have the testimony from every generation of Christians who have encountered the risen Christ in the deep consolations of prayer and in the transformation of our lives.

. . . .

PAUSE

Look back in thanksgiving over the last few days. Where have you met with and experienced the power of the resurrection?

. . . .

PRAY

Almighty Father, who in your great mercy gladdened the disciples with the sight of the risen Lord: give us such knowledge of his presence with us, that we may be strengthened and sustained by his risen life …
Collect for the Third Sunday of Easter

DAY 23
ASCENSION

READ Acts 1.1-11

'When he had said this, as they were watching, he was lifted up, and a cloud took him out of their sight.'

....

REFLECT

The tomb is empty but the throne is occupied.

These were the opening words of the most memorable sermon I've heard on the Ascension of Jesus. They capture brilliantly the truth that the doctrine of the Ascension is not about time and space (where Jesus is going when he is 'lifted up') but about our theological understanding.

Jesus is not in some kind of waiting room between his resurrection from the dead and his return as king. He is Lord, as the early Church will confess over and over again and reigns over the Church and the world. The kingdom is not yet come in all its fullness but the signs of the kingdom continue to break into the world.

'Jesus is seated' – that is enthroned – 'at the right hand of the Father'. As we proclaim this we draw on the great tradition of the Psalms which declare over and over again: 'The Lord is King' or 'The Lord reigns' (see Psalms 93 and 97 for examples).

. . . .

PAUSE

Lift up your eyes and your heart today and remember each hour that the Lord is King.

. . . .

PRAY

Grant, we pray, almighty God, that as we believe Jesus to have ascended into the heavens, so we in heart and mind may also ascend and with him continually dwell.
Collect for Ascension Day

DAY 24
TAKING STOCK

READ Luke 19.11-27

'I tell you, to all those who have, more will be given, but from those who have nothing, even what they have will be taken away.'

. . . .

REFLECT

Jesus is not in a waiting room until he returns and nor are we. The parable of the pounds catches the sense of purpose in the way we are to use the time that is given to us on this earth. These are the in between times, the times when the kingdom of God is breaking in. We are to take the immense treasure we have been given and invest it for profit and fruit for God's kingdom.

We are not all the same. Different people will be given different resources. Not every stage of life is the same either: the demands of work and family and opportunity for ministry will vary. But every person in every life stage is called to do what we can: to invest in others, to work for justice and peace, to dedicate each part of our lives to God, to consecrate our lives to God in holiness, to witness to the good news of God's love.

. . . .

PAUSE

Take stock of your life. How are you investing the treasure the Lord has entrusted to you at this stage of your life?

. . . .

PRAY

Grant us Lord,
the wisdom and the grace to use aright
the time that is left to us here on earth.
From the Funeral Service

WE ARE GOD'S POEM

READ Ephesians 2.1-10

'For we are what he has made us, created in Christ Jesus for good works, which God prepared beforehand to be our way of life.'

. . . .

REFLECT

Today's passage is deeply creedal. It summarizes the meaning of the death and resurrection of Jesus and the deep impact on our lives of this cosmic event. Verse 8 reminds us that it is by grace we have been saved through faith and this is not our own doing. We are reminded again of the power of declaring and resting our trust in God.

But verse 10 is my favourite. Ephesians describes what is happening now. We, the Church are God's creation: we are, literally, God's poem, the song God is singing to the world. This poem of creation is ongoing. Literally the meaning is: 'We are being created'. God is weaving and building the Church in the present through the work of the Spirit, the love of the Father and the presence of the risen Christ.

Is it not wonderful to be knitted into the story God is telling and the garment God is making as the pinnacle of creation? Together we are called into a relationship and dance of love with God the Trinity – a dance which will last for ever.

. . . .

PAUSE

Take time to reflect on the patterns God is weaving in your own life and in your own local church in this time.

. . . .

PRAY

Sev'n whole days, not one in sev'n,
I will praise Thee;
in my heart, though not in heav'n,
I can raise Thee.
Small it is, in this poor sort
to enroll Thee:
e'en eternity's too short
to extol Thee.
George Herbert

DAYS 26 TO 30
'I BELIEVE
IN THE
HOLY SPIRIT'

DAY 26
AS THE DEER

READ Psalm 42.1-6a

*'As the deer longs for the
waterbrooks, so longs my soul
for you, O God.'*

. . . .

REFLECT

As the creed unfolds we declare our faith and trust
first in the Father, the creator of heaven and earth
and next in the Son, Jesus Christ our Lord and
finally in the Holy Spirit, God's presence in the world
and in the life of every Christian.

We are made to know God and enjoy God for ever.

Our longing for God is compared in Psalm 42 to a thirsty deer's longing for streams of water in a parched desert landscape. This is a longing for water which refreshes, which cools, which gives life.

Our lives are incomplete and our hearts are restless without the presence of the Holy Spirit in our lives. One of the deepest joys of the Christian way is to know and recognize the presence of God, the fellowship with the Spirit, in the very depths of our being. The Spirit is the living water.

. . . .

PAUSE

Reflect on your life through the image of a desert or dry garden. Where are the deep wells of the Spirit's life?

. . . .

PRAY

Come creator Spirit, source of life;
sustain us when our hearts are heavy
and our wells have run dry,
for you are the Father's gift.
Common Worship Psalm Prayer
for Psalm 42

DAY 27
PENTECOST

READ Acts 2.1-11

'Divided tongues, as of fire, appeared among them and a tongue rested on each of them.'

. . . .

REFLECT

In Old Testament times, God's Spirit comes to rest on certain anointed individuals and for certain offices. The Spirit of God falls on prophets and teachers and craftsmen and kings for specific ministries and bringing certain gifts. But those same prophets speak of a time when God will pour out his Spirit on everyone – Peter will quote Joel's words at the beginning of his Pentecost sermon.

The Day of Pentecost is that very moment when the Holy Spirit is poured out on God's Church. Luke's account deploys the beautiful metaphors of wind and fire, and stresses through the divided tongues and the gifts given that the Spirit is now given to every believer.

This remains the faith of the Church, declared in the creed: we are each anointed and filled with the Spirit of God who calls us into life, gives us gifts for Christian service and assures us of God's presence in the different seasons of our lives.

. . . .

PAUSE

In which seasons of your life have you been especially aware of the presence of the Holy Spirit? In which has the Spirit seemed to be absent?

. . . .

PRAY

O God, the King of glory... we beseech you, leave us not comfortless, but send your Holy Spirit to strengthen us...
Collect for the Sunday after Ascension Day

THE GIFTS OF THE SPIRIT

READ 1 Corinthians 12.1-13

'Now there are varieties of gifts, but the same Spirit; and there are varieties of services, but the same Lord.'

. . . .

REFLECT

The Church is one. But the Spirit gives different gifts for different kinds of service within the one Church. This leads in turn to a key question: are some people or gifts or ministries more important than others in the life of the Church?

Paul's answer to the Corinthians is an emphatic no to all three questions. He uses the image of the human body. The body is one. The body has many different parts (members). They are of equal value and their difference is essential to the good working of the body.

In the same way the same Spirit is given to every member of the Church, the Body of Christ. All are of equal value. These gifts are very different. There are several lists in the New Testament and none is definitive. No one has them all. We are called to love and to honour one another and we need each other.

. . . .

PAUSE

What gifts have you been given and what service are you called to offer? How much do you value those gifts in relation to the gifts of others?

. . . .

PRAY

Almighty and everlasting God, by whose Spirit the whole body of the Church is governed and sanctified: hear our prayer which we offer for all your faithful people, that in their vocation and ministry they may serve you in holiness and truth.
Collect for the Fifth Sunday after Trinity

THE PROMISE
OF THE SPIRIT

READ John 16.12-15

'I still have many things to say to you, but you cannot bear them now.'

. . . .

REFLECT

Jesus' love and care for his disciples is clear from every part of the discourses set down in John 12-17. They begin with Jesus washing his disciples' feet. They end with Jesus' prayer for unity for those he loves: 'that the love with which you have loved me may be in them, and I in them.' (17.26).

We are invited to join this intimate relationship of love in which Jesus makes his home within us, by the Spirit of God. One of the reasons the Spirit is given is to guide the disciples into all truth.

We learn slowly. This applies to the twelve in the upper room who could not hear or bear all that Jesus has to say to them. It applies to Christians today who have much to learn over all our lives. It applies to the Church which needs to learn and relearn the truths at the heart of the faith. The Spirit is given to be our teacher within and to glorify Jesus.

. . . .

PAUSE

Look back over your Christian life and the life of the Church as you know it. Where has the Spirit been leading you and the Church into all truth?

. . . .

PRAY

God, who as at this time
taught the hearts of your faithful people
by sending them the light
of your Holy Spirit:
grant us by the same Spirit
to have a right judgement in all things ...
Collect for Pentecost Sunday

LISTEN TO THE SPIRIT

READ Revelation 2.1-7

'Let anyone who has an ear listen to what the Spirit is saying to the Churches.'

. . . .

REFLECT

The Book of Revelation begins with a stunning vision of Christ and continues with seven short letters written to the Churches of Asia. The letters are all distinctive: they address specific spiritual conditions or dangers in one place and time. They are all similar as well and pick up different elements in the vision of Christ and promises for the future.

The letters are bound together by a refrain and a plea: 'Listen to what the Spirit is saying to the Churches'. Here too is a vital insight into the work of the Spirit and the Christian Way. Disciples are those who are called to listen. We listen as we read the Scriptures. We listen also for the voice of the Spirit as we discern which way to go, the priorities on our lives, the calling of the Church.

Each time we say the Apostles' Creed we make the solemn declaration: I believe in the Holy Spirit. To say these words is to commit ourselves afresh to this work of listening.

. . . .

PAUSE

What do you believe the Spirit is saying to the Church today? How will you test what you believe God is saying with others?

. . . .

PRAY

Almighty God,
who sent your Holy Spirit
to be the life and light of your Church:
open our hearts to the riches of your grace
that we may bring forth
the fruit of the Spirit
in love and joy and peace …
Collect for the Ninth Sunday after Trinity

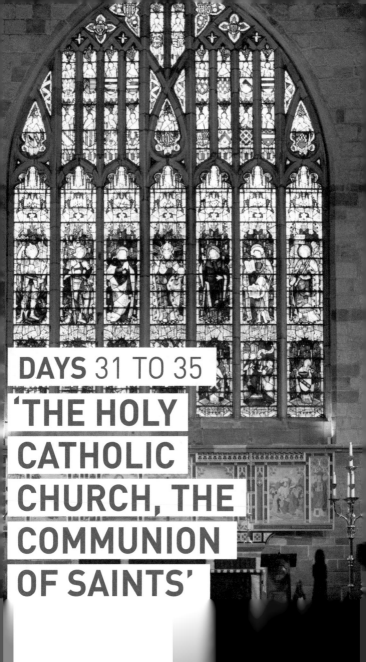

DAYS 31 TO 35

'THE HOLY CATHOLIC CHURCH, THE COMMUNION OF SAINTS'

DAY 31
THE PEOPLE OF GOD

READ Psalm 1

'Like a tree planted by streams of water bearing fruit in due season, with leaves that do not wither, whatever they do, it shall prosper.'

. . . .

REFLECT

Christians believe amazing things. Out of all the nations of the earth, all the people who have ever lived, God has called a people for himself. The call and invitation came first to a family, then a nation and then through Jesus Christ to all the nations in every age.

God calls us into this community through baptism which signifies being washed and forgiven and also dying to our old life and rising to new life in Christ. Through baptism we are grafted into the tree planted by streams of living water, the holy and catholic Church. Holy means set apart and sanctified by God's grace. Catholic means for the whole world.

The Church is not a community in waiting but a community with a purpose: to bear fruit for God's kingdom – the fruit of justice, the fruit of Christ-like qualities in our lives and the fruit of a harvest of new Christians in every generation.

PAUSE

Remember today with thanksgiving your own baptism and those who brought you to faith and to be part of God's church.

PRAY

Christ our wisdom, give us delight in your law that we may bear fruits of patience and peace in the kingdom of the righteous; for your mercy's sake.
Common Worship Psalm Prayer for Psalm 1

CALLED WITH A PURPOSE

READ Mark 3.13-19a

*'And Jesus appointed twelve …
to be with him and to be sent out … '*

. . . .

REFLECT

Today's reading from Mark offers one of the earliest descriptions of the Church in the New Testament. The twelve disciples echo the twelve tribes of Israel. This is the beginning of the new people of God. We are called by Jesus rather than choosing to join an organisation. We are called with a purpose: to be with him (together) and to be sent out.

This one short phrase sets the entire rhythm of the life of God's Church. We come together to be with Jesus and we are sent out. It is the rhythm of the two greatest commandments: we come together to offer our love to God and we are sent out to love our neighbours. It is the rhythm of the great sacrament of the Eucharist: we come together to be fed and nurtured by our Lord and we are sent out to love and heal the world.

We are the Church gathered on Sundays. But we are the Church dispersed on every day of the week bearing fruit for the kingdom of our Lord.

. . . .

PAUSE

Can you see this rhythm clearly in the life of your local church? If not, how can it be strengthened?

. . . .

PRAY

God, the giver of life,
whose Holy Spirit wells up
within your Church:
by the Spirit's gifts equip us
to live the gospel of Christ
and make us eager to do your will ...
Collect for the Twentieth Sunday after
Trinity

DAY 33
LIFE AMONG THE BELIEVERS

READ Acts 2.37-47

'They devoted themselves to the apostles' teaching and fellowship, to the breaking of bread and the prayers.'

. . . .

REFLECT

The early Church sets a loved and normative pattern for the Church in every generation. We enter the Church like every generation of Christians through repentance for our sins and faith in Jesus Christ; through baptism in water and as we receive the gift of the Holy Spirit and our life is joined to God's life in a new and deeper way.

With the Church in every generation, we devote ourselves to the ways in which we grow stronger and deeper in that faith: the apostles' teaching expressed in the Scriptures, to fellowship, the common life of the Church, to the sacrament of the Eucharist and also to meals eaten together and to prayer.

This beginning and this pattern of devotion and the inner life bears fruit in the wider community, in healing, in the relief of poverty and in the remarkable expansion and growth of the early Christian communities.

. . . .

PAUSE

Examine your own life and practice. Are you devoted to the teaching of the apostles, to fellowship, to the breaking of bread and to the prayers?

. . . .

PRAY

God, who in generous mercy sent the Holy Spirit upon your Church in the burning fire of your love: grant that your people may be fervent in the fellowship of the gospel that, always abiding in you, they may be found steadfast in faith and active in service ...
Collect for the Fifteenth Sunday after Trinity

THE WORSHIP OF HEAVEN

READ Revelation 7.9-17

'For the Lamb at the centre of the throne will be their shepherd, and he will guide them to springs of the water of life, and God will wipe away every tear from their eyes ... '

. . . .

REFLECT

According to The Pilgrim Way (see p. 99 of this booklet), the Church is 'the pilgrim people of God, the body of Christ and the community of disciples in every age in earth and heaven'. The Book of Revelation draws back the curtain and allows us to see the community of saints. The emphasis here is on the suffering of the Church in every age: the Christian way is a costly one as we have seen.

The Church in heaven is joined with the Church on earth in the eternal worship of God, Father, Son and Holy Spirit. The Church in heaven continues in prayer and intercession for the Church here on earth. The earthly lives of the saints continue to inspire us whether they are Christians from the past who have lived holy lives dedicated to God or people we have known in the present who reflect in some way the grace and love of God to us. We need one another.

. . . .

PAUSE

Who are the saints who have inspired you from the long story of the Church and the people you have met?

. . . .

PRAY

Almighty and eternal God,
you have kindled the flame of love
in the hearts of the saints:
grant to us the same faith
and power of love,
that, as we rejoice in their triumphs,
we may be sustained
by their example and fellowship …
Collect for the Fourth Sunday before Advent

DAY 35
THE GREAT COMMISSION

READ Matthew 28.16-20

'Go therefore and make disciples of all nations, baptizing them … and teaching them to obey everything that I have commanded you.'

. . . .

REFLECT

Jesus gives to his disciples a clear mission to make new disciples: they are to share the good news and draw others into the Christian community through baptism. The Nicene Creed adds two marks of the Church to 'holy' and 'catholic'. The Church is called to be one. The Church is called to be 'apostolic': built on the foundation of the apostles but also sent into all the world as the apostles are sent.

In the original text 'make disciples' is the central commission here. The other verbs are all participles: going, baptizing and teaching. These all become central activities of the Church in the great missionary endeavour.

We are not called simply to wait for people to come to us but to go to where they are. We are called to offer the whole of the good news. Baptism and teaching must be joined together to see Christ formed in every Christian and every Christian grow to maturity.

. . . .

PAUSE

How are you called to engage in this great commission to make disciples?

. . . .

PRAY

Almighty God, who called your Church to witness that you were in Christ reconciling the world to yourself: help us so to proclaim the good news of your love, that all who hear it may be drawn to you …
Collect for Mission and Evangelism

DAYS 36 TO 40

'THE FORGIVENESS OF SINS, THE RESURRECTION OF THE BODY AND THE LIFE EVERLASTING'

THE FORGIVENESS OF SINS

READ Psalm 32.1-7

'Happy is the one whose transgression is forgiven, and whose sin is covered.'

. . . .

REFLECT

It is sometimes a difficult thing to realize that we are not perfect. But it is enormously liberating to realize first that imperfection is part of the human condition and, second, that God stands ready to forgive.

God's forgiveness is readily available 24 hours a day, 7 days a week and 365 days a year. God's forgiveness is available through the whole length of our lives. Forgiveness is retrospective over the whole course of our lives. Our actions are covered as well as our words, our thoughts and our intentions.

There is nothing we can do to earn this forgiveness: no accumulation of good deeds, no vows or promises, no sacrifices. God's forgiveness is a generous gift of grace, made possible once and for all through the death of the Son of God on the cross.

This good news of forgiveness is not only for me or for those around me as I say the creed. It is my calling to make it known.

PAUSE

Who around me most needs to know about God's forgiveness? What is the next step in helping them to understand it?

PRAY

Give us honest hearts, O God, and send your kindly Spirit to help us confess our sins and bring us the peace of your forgiveness...
Common Worship Psalm Prayer for Psalm 32

DAY 37
CONFESSION

READ Matthew 11.25-30

'Come to me, all you that are weary and are carrying heavy burdens, and I will give you rest.'

. . . .

REFLECT

The old Prayer Book service of Holy Communion is fundamentally pastoral: threaded through the service are powerful reminders of God's love. At the very centre of the service stand the 'Comfortable Words': Matthew 11.28 followed by John 3.16; 1 Timothy 1.15 and 1 John 2.1. They are read after the confession and absolution, reminders of the power of Christian assurance: we really do believe in the forgiveness of sins – even our own.

John Bunyan in *The Pilgrim's Progress* picks up Jesus' theme of carrying heavy burdens in his image of Christian becoming aware of the great burden of sin upon his back, weighing down his every step. In Bunyan's great allegory, Christian comes at last to the cross. The burden on his back rolls away for ever. Christian is set free.

Radical forgiveness affects not only our eternal destiny but our lived experience. There is no need to carry the burdens of shame and guilt for past misdeeds. They are gone, by the grace of God. We are forgiven.

. . . .

PAUSE

Make an act of confession of all that is troubling you and seek God's forgiveness.

. . . .

PRAY

Grant, we beseech you, merciful Lord, to your faithful people pardon and peace, that they may be cleansed from all their sins and serve you with a quiet mind …
Collect for the Twenty-first Sunday after Trinity

THE RESURRECTION OF THE BODY

READ 1 Corinthians 15.50-58

'Therefore, my beloved, be steadfast, immovable, always excelling in the work of the Lord, because you know that in the Lord your labour is not in vain.'

. . . .

REFLECT

The benefits of God's forgiveness are immense. But Paul makes clear earlier in 1 Corinthians 15: 'If for this life only we have hoped in Christ, we are of all people most to be pitied' (verse 18).

Christians trust and hope that there will be resurrection from the dead not to a physical body but to a spiritual body. We will not be re-absorbed into the cosmos. We will not be disembodied souls. We will be distinctive beings within creation, raised to be with Christ for ever. The analogy of the seed in verse 37 is helpful: it is impossible to look at an acorn and imagine an oak tree. So it is impossible to understand or to picture the resurrection body.

We place our trust in this most powerful of promises for good reason, because of the resurrection of Jesus from the dead, which we have already declared. And the effect on our lives: to make us steadfast and immovable, always abounding in the work of the Lord.

. . . .

PAUSE

The prospect of death makes us anxious and afraid. Where do you need to steady the ship of faith at the present time and restore your sense of being steadfast and immovable?

. . . .

PRAY

Almighty God, who through your only begotten Son Jesus Christ have overcome death and opened to us the gate of everlasting life: grant that, as by your grace going before us you put into our minds good desires, so by your continual help we may bring them to good effect …
Collect for the Fifth Sunday after Easter

THE LIFE EVERLASTING

READ Acts 8.26-40

'Look, here is water! What is to prevent me from being baptized?'

. . . .

REFLECT

The themes of the Apostles' Creed come together in the powerful story of the Ethiopian eunuch. Here is someone whose race and identity seem to put him beyond the reach of God's love. But God speaks to him through the Scriptures, through sending Philip and through the good news of Jesus, and calls him to new life.

The eunuch seeks baptism: the sign of washing and cleansing, the sign of death to our old selves and rising to new life. One of the ancient alternative texts of the Acts of the Apostles inserts a short confession of faith (found in the margins of most translations): If you believe with all your heart, you may. And he replied: "I believe that Jesus Christ is the Son of God." '

This is the kernel of the creed, deployed at the point of baptism and down all the years to come. To speak these words is to step back into the experience of baptism: the forgiveness of sins, the resurrection from the dead and the life everlasting.

PAUSE

How are you called to live out your baptism in this season of your life? Is there someone with whom you might have a conversation to review this?

PRAY

Heavenly Father, by the power of your Holy Spirit you give your faithful people new life in the water of baptism. Guide and strengthen us by the same Spirit, that we who are born again may serve you in faith and love, and grow into the full stature of your Son, Jesus Christ.
Common Worship Collect for Baptism

DAY 40
LISTEN TO HIM

READ Matthew 17.1-8

'This is my Son, the Beloved,
with whom I am well pleased.'

. . . .

REFLECT

Christians believe amazing and beautiful things.
As we say the creed, we rehearse these truths,
we claim them and return to them and live in them
in new ways. The different lines of the creed take us
to the beginning and end of creation, to the mutual
love of the Trinity, to the mystery of the Church,
to the life-giving work of the Spirit.

But at the very centre of the creed and of our
discipleship is Jesus Christ. It is Jesus who reveals to

us the nature of God and Jesus who reveals to us what it means to be human.

There will be days and seasons in our lives when we are able to hold in our minds the whole breadth and depth of our salvation and the wideness of God's mercy. But there will be days and seasons in our lives when only one thing matters. When those days come, let this be what you remember: 'This is my Son, the Beloved ...' Listen to him.

PAUSE

Look back over this journey of 40 days. What are you taking with you? What will be the next steps on your journey of daily prayer?

PRAY

Almighty Father, whose Son was revealed in majesty before he suffered death upon the cross: give us grace to perceive his glory, that we may be strengthened to suffer with him and be changed into his likeness from glory to glory ...
Collect for the Sunday next before Lent

NEXT STEPS

pilgrim
A COURSE FOR THE CHRISTIAN JOURNEY

JOIN A LOCAL GROUP USING THE 'PILGRIM' COURSE

Pilgrim: A Course for the Christian Journey is widely used across and beyond the Church of England. *Pilgrim* offers eight short courses designed to be used by small groups of people who are exploring the Christian faith. The course is based around four core texts, including The Creeds. Find out more about *Pilgrim* books, eBooks, DVDs and online resources at **www.pilgrimcourse.org**

. . . .

EXPLORE OTHER *PILGRIM JOURNEY* BOOKLETS

Other booklets in this series include *Pilgrim Journeys: The Lord's Prayer* and *Pilgrim Journeys: The Beatitudes*, both published in 2020. A future volume on *The Commandments* is expected during 2021.

. . . .

JOIN IN WITH FURTHER DISCIPLESHIP CAMPAIGNS

Visit **www.churchofengland.org** to sign up to take part in future discipleship initiatives from the Church of England. It is free to sign up and you can easily opt out at any time.

. . . .

TAKE PART IN
THY KINGDOM COME

Thy Kingdom Come is a global prayer movement that invites Christians around the world to pray for more people to come to know Jesus.

What started in 2016 as an invitation from the Archbishops of Canterbury and York to the Church of England has grown into an international and ecumenical call to prayer.

During the 11 days of ***Thy Kingdom Come*** – between Ascension and Pentecost – it is hoped that everyone who participates will deepen their friendship with Jesus, bring others to know Jesus or know him better, and come to know that every aspect of their life is the stuff of prayer.

For more details and a wide range of resources visit **www.thykingdomcome.global**

. . . .